Crock Pot Cookbook

50 High Protein Delicious Recipes That Guarantee Weight Loss

Luca Bucciarelli

© **Copyright 2017 by Luca Bucciarelli**
All rights reserved.

This document is geared towards providing exact and reliable information in regards to the topic and issue covered. The publication is sold with the idea that the publisher is not required to render accounting, officially permitted, or otherwise, qualified services. If advice is necessary, legal or professional, a practiced individual in the profession should be ordered.

- From a Declaration of Principles which was accepted and approved equally by a Committee of the American Bar Association and a Committee of Publishers and Associations.

In no way is it legal to reproduce, duplicate, or transmit any part of this document in either electronic means or in printed format. Recording of this publication is strictly prohibited and any storage of this document is not allowed unless with written permission from the publisher. All rights reserved.

The information provided herein is stated to be truthful and consistent, in that any liability, in terms of inattention or otherwise, by any usage or abuse of any policies, processes, or directions contained within is the solitary and utter responsibility of the recipient reader. Under no circumstances will any legal responsibility or blame be held against the publisher for any reparation, damages, or monetary loss due to the information herein, either directly or indirectly.

Respective authors own all copyrights not held by the publisher.

The information herein is offered for informational purposes solely, and is universal as so. The presentation of the information is without contract or any type of guarantee assurance.

The trademarks that are used are without any consent, and the publication of the trademark is without permission or backing by the trademark owner. All trademarks and brands within this book are for clarifying purposes only and are the owned by the owners themselves, not affiliated with this document.

Table of Contents

INTRODUCTION — VII
CHAPTER 1: CROCKPOT 101 — 1
Size of the Crockpot — 1
Removable Inner Pot — 2
Heat Settings — 2
Faster Cooking — 2
CHAPTER 2: THE BENEFITS OF SLOW COOKING — 3
Delicious and Nutritious meals — 4
Saves time — 4
Always useful — 4
Lesser Energy Consumption — 4
Very Easy to Clean — 5
Portable — 5
Tips and Tricks — 5
CHAPTER 3: MEAL PLAN — 7
CHAPTER 4: RECIPES FOR BREAKFAST — 10
1. Spinach and Mushroom Quiche — 10
2. Pepperoncini Beef Sandwiches — 12
3. Breakfast Oatmeal — 13
4. Carrot Cake and Zucchini Bread Oatmeal — 15
5. Buckwheat porridge — 16
6. Tortillas — 17
7. Apple Cherry Breakfast Risotto — 19
8. Shrimp and Artichoke Barley Risotto — 21
9. Cinnamon Swirl Slow cooked Pancake Bake — 23
CHAPTER 5: RECIPES FOR SOUPS AND STEWS — 24
10. Chicken and Pasta Soup — 24
11. Pork Chop Soup — 26

12. Lentil Soup --- 28
13. Creamy Crab Soup -- 30
14. Autumn Vegetable Beef Stew ------------------------------------- 32
15. Turkey Chili -- 34
16. Fisherman Stew --- 35
CHAPTER 6: RECIPES FOR CHICKEN ----------------------------------- 37
17. Buffalo Ranch Chicken Sandwiches ----------------------------- 37
18. Hawaiian Chicken --- 38
19. Sweet n Sour Chicken -- 40
20. Peachy Barbecue Chicken -- 41
21. Chicken Curry in a Hurry -- 42
CHAPTER 7: RECIPES FOR TURKEY -------------------------------------- 43
22. Turkey Casserole --- 43
23. Mediterranean Roast Turkey ------------------------------------ 45
24. Sesame Ginger Turkey Wraps ----------------------------------- 47
25. Slow cooked Herby Turkey Breast ----------------------------- 49
26. Turkey Pad Thai -- 51
CHAPTER 8: RECIPES FOR BEEF -- 53
27. Beef Tacos -- 53
28. Cauliflower Beef --- 55
29. Pot Roast --- 57
30. Beef Roast --- 59
CHAPTER 9: RECIPES FOR PORK -- 60
31. Pork Roast --- 60
32. Spicy Pulled Pork -- 62
33. Pork Chops -- 64
34. Super Easy Country Style Ribs --------------------------------- 66
CHAPTER 10: RECIPES FOR LAMB -------------------------------------- 67
35. Lamb with Garlic -- 67
36. Herbed Lamb -- 69
37. Moroccan Lamb --- 71
38. Slow Cooked Leg of Lamb -------------------------------------- 73

39. Shredded Lamb --- 75
CHAPTER 11: RECIPES FOR SEAFOOD --- 77
40. Seafood Stew --- 77
41. Seafood Curry --- 79
42. Tuna Casserole --- 81
43. Crockpot Cheese and Prawns --- 83
CHAPTER 12: RECIPES FOR DESSERTS --- 85
44. Crunchy Cheesecake --- 85
45. Chocolate Pudding Cake --- 87
46. Blueberry Cake --- 89
47. Crispy Apples --- 91
48. Coconut Rice Pudding --- 92
49. Pear Caramel Pudding --- 93
50. Tapioca Pudding --- 95
51. Mini Salted Caramel Mocha Cheesecakes --- 97
FINAL WORDS --- 99

Introduction

Time is not a great friend to most people. You may wake up one morning and decide to cook a healthy meal for yourself and will go about getting the ingredients ready and will just begin to cook and realize that you have no time left. You need to rush to get ready for work or get your kids ready for school. What do you do in times like these? You need to provide your family and yourself a meal that is healthy and balanced. This is where a crockpot becomes your best friend. You can provide your family with delicious meals at all times of the day using a crockpot.

This book provides information on how a crockpot is helpful and also a few tips that will help you on your way. There are 50 high protein recipes that are delicious and succulent and will leave you asking for more.

Thank you for purchasing the book. I hope you enjoy the recipes.

Chapter 1: Crockpot 101

When you have a busy schedule, a deadline approaching at work or your kid's school project to complete, how would you find time to prepare a healthy meal? This is where the crock-pot comes in.

You will be able to make nutritious meals using the crockpot. You will initially be surprised at how easy it is to cook with a crock-pot, and will then probably begin to wonder why you had not done this earlier. After all of that, you will be able to focus on cooking these meals that are delicious and healthy too.

Do you know what the best part of this crockpot is? You will be able to save time and also make nutritious meals for your family, but the greatest part about this is that you will finally be able to lose the excess weight that you have been trying to lose. You will never have to even cook when you use a crockpot. This is the beauty of a crockpot that comes with a timer. This appliance will cook your food while you go about your work and will turn off when the food has been prepared.

When you are willing to enter into the world of crockpots, you will need to keep a few things in mind. It is always good not to leave things to chance and I am sure most people can relate to this.

Size of the Crockpot

This is of great essence since you will need to buy a crockpot that will suffice for your family. If you are a family of four, you will be able to work with a 3 – quarts crockpot. If you have a larger family, you will need to use a larger sized crockpot. Like every other appliance, you cannot decide on which one is the best crockpot that you can use. You will need to find the appropriate one for your family.

Removable Inner Pot

Every crockpot has an inner pot that is removable and one, which can be used to serve food. There are certain brands that have this part made from an aluminum cast, which makes it easier to sear different kinds of meat in the crockpot itself. You would not have to use a stove to sear the meat. But, the thing to remember is that aluminum is not a very safe metal to use to cook since the temperatures increase inside the pot. The important thing to remember is that a crockpot is based on cooking with low heat.

Heat Settings

Every crockpot has different heat settings. There are some that only function well on lower heat settings while there are others that function well on the very same settings. You should always read the reviews of the different crockpots that you have shortlisted on. Make sure that you understand how the warm setting that is in this crockpot works. This setting is of great importance since it keeps your food warm after it has been cooked well. If this setting is not there in the crockpot, it will switch off automatically

Faster Cooking

Crockpots can work without any supervision and prepare food for close to eight hours. There are some crockpots that can allow you to prepare these meals within a few hours without having to wait for too long. But, it is always good to avoid preparing food this way since a crockpot is all about cooking slowly to preserve the nutrition.

You need to remember to learn how to use a crockpot irrespective of how many settings may be available in this appliance.

Chapter 2: The Benefits of Slow Cooking

You may have heard a lot of people tell you about how great a crockpot is but would never have considered purchasing one. When you own a crockpot of a good brand, you will find all your cooking fantasies come true. You would not have to stand in front of a hot stove and cook for hours after a long day of work. Imagine how great it would be if you came into the house to the smell of a slowly cooked chicken or herb cooked salmon? That would definitely be heaven would it not? You will be able to cook meals that are nutritious and healthy and would also be able to spend lesser time in front of the stove.

After having read all this, you may probably be under the impression that you would not have to do anything. But, there is some prep that you will need to make in order to have a lot of healthy and nutritious meals. You may need to brown the meat on the stovetop and may need to chop and dice your vegetables before you put them inside the crockpot. Once all the prep is done, you will just need to put all the vegetables and the other ingredients into the crockpot and just go about your day. You will come back home to a well-prepared meal.

The best part about a crockpot is that the meal will be ready in no time and if it is ready faster than you anticipated, you will find that the pot has moved to the warm mode and has preserved your food the way it should be. Let's take a look at a few more benefits of cooking with a crockpot.

Delicious and Nutritious meals

The ingredients are all fresh and cooked at low temperatures for a longer period of time. Since the vegetables and other ingredients are all cooked slowly, and are not subjected to too much heat, the nutrients will be preserved in these ingredients. All the juices in the vegetables will also remain intact, which would make the food more succulent and delicious.

Saves time

When you cook using a stovetop, you will be spending hours to ensure that the ingredients you are using are cooked to perfection. But, when it comes to a crockpot, you will not have to worry since you will only need to do the initial prep. Your crockpot will take care of everything else for you. You can go about doing what you would normally do.

Always useful

You would never have to worry about when you can use a crockpot to make meals since they are season friendly. You can use these appliances any time of the year! The advantage of a crockpot is that it eliminates the need to use an oven and also prevents your house from heating up too much.

Lesser Energy Consumption

You will find that a crockpot uses substantially lesser amounts of energy when compared with an electric oven.

Very Easy to Clean

You would only need to clean up the cutting board, a knife and maybe the pan that you have used to brown the meat you will be cooking. Apart from that you will only need to clean the crockpot as opposed to cleaning multiple utensils.

Portable

A crockpot is easy to transfer. You will not have the need to transfer the meal onto a serving plate if you do not want to.

When you shop for a crockpot, you will have to always factor in the number of people you will be cooking for. You will be able to prepare lovely meals using a crockpot. You need to remember to care for your crockpot too. Let us take a look at a few tips that will come in handy when you are using a crockpot to make your meals.

Tips and Tricks

If you are a little skeptical of preparing meals in the crockpot when you are away from home, you can easily find different meals to substitute. You can cook meals overnight and not worry about burning the house down since this electric appliance is user friendly and will turn off the minute the food has cooked fully.

> When you need to clean the crockpot, you will need to just rub the inside of the crockpot with oil or a cooking spray that will not stick to the insides. It is always easy to clean the liners of the crockpot, but you will need to make sure that you do it often to avoid messing the crockpot up.

Before you cook any frozen poultry or meat, you will need to bring them down to room temperature to ensure that the meat is cooked through fully. You can brown them on a stovetop before you put them inside the cooker.

Always make sure that you only fill two thirds of the cooker. You need to remember that if you cook too little and too much in the crockpot, you will be affecting the cooking time and the quality of the food.

Since the vegetables usually take longer to cook when compared to meat and other poultry, you should cook them first. Place the meat in the crockpot over the vegetables and top them with a broth, sauce or water.

You will need to add the broth, barbecue sauce or water to the crockpot depending on the recipe you are using. Since the sauces take longer to reduce, you can cook them for longer in the crockpot to reduce.

If you find it easier, you can set the crockpot on high for the first one hour and then turn the heat lower to finish cooking.

Always keep the lid of the crockpot in place when you are cooking. If you keep moving the lid of the crockpot, you will be losing out on the cooking time.

Always add the pasta and other grains to the crockpot only in the end to avoid having a mushy dish. The other option could be to cook these pastas and grains separately and only add them to the dish before you serve.

Always add cream and milk only in the last half an hour to avoid the curdling of these dairy products.

When it comes to soft vegetables, you can add them only during the last half an hour of the cooking process.

Always check up on your dish when half the cooking time is done. You do not necessarily have to but it is good to do this.

Chapter 3: Meal plan

In this chapter, I have devised a 15-day meal plan, which can be doubled as a 30-day plan. You can swap recipes, as long as you stick to any of the recipes from the book.

DAYS	BREAKFAST	LUNCH	SNACK	DINNER	DESSERT
Day 1	Breakfast - Pepperoncini Beef Sandwiches	Lunch – Buffalo Ranch Chicken Sandwiches	Snack - Chicken and Pasta Soup	Dinner – Herbed Lamb	Desserts - Crunchy Cheesecake
Day 2	Breakfast - Breakfast Oatmeal	Lunch – Mediterranean Roast Turkey	Snack - Beef Tacos	Dinner – Spicy Pulled Pork	Desserts - Blueberry Cake
Day 3	Breakfast - Spinach and Mushroom Quiche	Lunch – Pot Roast	Snack - Pork Chop Soup	Dinner – Turkey Casserole	Desserts - Chocolate Pudding Cake
Day 4	Breakfast - Buckwheat Porridge	Lunch – Turkey Pad Thai	Snack - Creamy Crab Soup	Dinner – Crockpot Cheese and Prawns	Desserts - Crispy Apples
Day 5	Breakfast - Carrot Cake and Zucchini Bread Oatmeal	Lunch – Beef Roast	Snack - Fisherman Stew	Dinner – Super Easy Country Style Ribs	Desserts - Coconut Rice Pudding

Day 6	Breakfast - Apple Cherry Breakfast Risotto	Lunch – Sweet n Sour Chicken	Snack - Turkey Chili	Dinner – Pork Chops	Desserts - Mini Salted Caramel Mocha Cheesecakes
Day 7	Breakfast - Cinnamon Swirl Slow cooked Pancake Bake	Lunch – Seafood Curry	Snack - Autumn Vegetable Beef Stew	Dinner – Sesame Ginger Turkey Wraps	Desserts - Pear Caramel Pudding
Day 8	Breakfast - Shrimp and Artichoke Barley Risotto	Lunch – Crockpot Cheese and Prawns	Snack - Chicken and Pasta Soup	Dinner – Slow cooked Herby Turkey Breast	Desserts - Blueberry Cake
Day 9	Breakfast - Breakfast Oatmeal	Lunch – Cauliflower Beef	Snack - Lentil Soup	Dinner – Tuna Casserole	Desserts - Tapioca Pudding
Day 10	Breakfast - Buckwheat Porridge	Lunch – Spicy Pulled Pork	Snack - Creamy Crab Soup	Dinner – Hawaiian Chicken	Desserts - Crunchy Cheesecake
Day 11	Breakfast - Spinach and Mushroom Quiche	Lunch – Lamb with Garlic	Snack - Pork Chop Soup	Dinner – Buffalo Ranch Chicken Sandwiches	Desserts - Coconut Rice Pudding
Day 12	Breakfast - Carrot Cake and Zucchini Bread Oatmeal	Lunch – Chicken Curry in a Hurry	Snack - Fisherman Stew	Dinner – Pork Roast	Desserts - Blueberry Cake

Day 13	Breakfast - Cinnamon Swirl Slow cooked Pancake Bake	Lunch – Shredded Lamb	Snack - Lentil Soup	Dinner – Slow cooked Herby Turkey Breast	Desserts - Mini Salted Caramel Mocha Cheesecakes
Day 14	Breakfast - Pepperoncini Beef Sandwiches	Lunch – Peachy Barbecue Chicken	Snack - Autumn Vegetable Beef Stew	Dinner – Moroccan Lamb	Desserts - Crispy Apples
Day 15	Breakfast - Breakfast Oatmeal	Lunch – Slow Cooked Leg of Lamb	Snack - Turkey Chili	Dinner – Pot Roast	Desserts - Chocolate Pudding Cake

Chapter 4: Recipes for Breakfast

1. Spinach and Mushroom Quiche

Ingredients:

3 1/2 cups frozen spinach

4 slices bacon, cooked crisp, crumbled

1 tablespoon olive oil

2 cups button mushrooms, chopped

1/2 cup red bell pepper, chopped

1 1/2 cups Swiss cheese or any other cheese, shredded

8 eggs

2 cups whole milk

2 tablespoons fresh chives, snipped

Salt to taste

Pepper to taste

1/2 cup packaged biscuit mix

1 disposable slow cooker liner

Cooking spray

Method:

Line the crockpot with the disposable liner.

Spray inside of the pot with cooking spray.

Squeeze the excess liquid from the spinach and place on paper towels.

Place a skillet with oil over medium heat. Add mushroom and bell pepper. Sauté until tender. Add spinach and cheese.

Meanwhile, in a bowl add eggs, milk, chives, salt and pepper. Whisk well.

Pour the egg mixture into the spinach mixture.

Add the biscuit mix and stir gently. Remove from heat and pour this mixture into the lined slow cooker.

Sprinkle bacon on top.

Cover and set the slow cooker on Low and cook for 4-5 hours or on High for 2-2 1/2 hours or a toothpick when inserted in the center should come out clean.

Cool for 15-20 minutes before serving. Slice into wedges and serve.

2. Pepperoncini Beef Sandwiches

Ingredients:

    1 1/2 pounds beef chuck roast
    2 cloves garlic, sliced
    1/2 jar (8 ounce) pepperoncini
    4 hoagie rolls, split lengthwise
    8 slices provolone cheese
    Salt to taste
    Pepper powder to taste

Method:

Make small slits in the roast.

Insert the garlic slices in the slits.

Place the roast in a crockpot. Add the pepperoncini along with the liquid over the meat.

Cover and set on Low for 6-8 hours.

Place meat in rolls along with the pepperoncini.

Sprinkle salt and pepper and top with cheese.

Microwave for a few seconds until the cheese melts and serve.

3. Breakfast Oatmeal

Ingredients:

1 cup walnuts + extra for topping
1 cup almonds + extra for topping
2 medium butternut squash, peeled, chopped into pieces
4 apples, cored, peeled, chopped into pieces
2 tablespoons coconut sugar or to taste (optional)
2 cups coconut milk + extra for topping or any other milk of your choice
2-3 tablespoons desiccated coconut
2 teaspoons cinnamon powder
½ teaspoon nutmeg powder
Maple syrup for topping (optional)

Method:

Soak the almonds and walnuts in a bowl of water to which a large pinch of sea salt is added, for about 10 – 12 hours. Drain and blend in a blender until smooth.

Add the blended nuts and rest of the ingredients to the crockpot. Mix well.

Cover and set the crockpot on Low for about 8 hours.

When cooked, mash the ingredients with a potato masher.

To serve, top with coconut milk, nuts, desiccated coconut, and maple syrup if desired.

4. Carrot Cake and Zucchini Bread Oatmeal

Ingredients:

1 small zucchini, peeled, grated
1 large carrot, peeled, grated
1 cup steel cut oats
1/2 cup pecans, chopped
1/8 teaspoon ground cloves
1/8 teaspoon ground nutmeg
3/4 teaspoon ground cinnamon
2 teaspoons vanilla extract
3 cups vanilla flavored milk
4 tablespoons agave nectar or maple syrup

Method:

Add all the ingredients except pecans to the crockpot at night and stir.

Cover and set on Low for 8 hours or on High for 4 hours.

Add pecans before serving. You can add more milk if you desire.

5. Buckwheat porridge

Ingredients
1 large cup of buckwheat groats
3 cups of rice or coconut milk
1 large ripe banana, sliced
1teaspoon cinnamon powder
1/teaspoon vanilla extract
¼ cup honey
¼ cup raisins
1/ cup freshly grated coconut
Some chopped walnuts

Method
1. Rinse some buckwheat and drain the water.
2. Add it to the instant pot. Pour some rice milk, sprinkle some cinnamon powder and add the vanilla extract. Mix well.
3. Simmer this mixture for about 2-3 minutes.
4. Throw in the grated coconut, raisins, ripened banana, add some honey and cover the lid of the instant pot.
5. Release the pressure slowly and remove the porridge in a large bowl.
6. Garnish with some chopped almond and serve.

6. Tortillas

Ingredients:
- 5 eggs
- 6 ounce Monterey Jack cheese, shredded
- 1 clove garlic, minced
- 1/2 cup half and half
- 1/2 a 4 ounce can chopped green chilies, drained
- 5 ounce taco sauce
- 1/4 teaspoon ancho chili powder
- 1/4 teaspoon black pepper powder
- Salt to taste
- 1 avocado, peeled, pitted, sliced
- 2 scallions, sliced
- 2 tablespoons fresh cilantro, chopped
- Juice of a lime
- Cooking spray
- 4 tortillas, warmed

Method:

Spray the inside of the crockpot with cooking spray.

Add eggs to a bowl and whisk well along with half and half, 4 ounces of cheese, pepper powder, salt, and chili powder. Add garlic and green chilies. Fold gently and transfer into the crockpot.

Cover and set on Low for 2 hours. Uncover and check after around 1 1/2 hours. If it is not set, then cook for another 30 minutes.

Pour taco sauce over the top of the set eggs and spread all over. Sprinkle the remaining cheese on top.

Cover and cook on Low for 15 minutes. Cut into 4-quarter pieces.

Place a piece over each of the tortillas. Sprinkle scallions and cilantro. Place avocado slices and finally sprinkle lemon juice and serve.

7. Apple Cherry Breakfast Risotto

Ingredients:
2 1/4 cups Arborio rice
3 large apples, cored, diced
3/4 cup dried cherries
3 tablespoons butter
3 teaspoons ground cinnamon
1/2 teaspoon salt or to taste
1/2 cup brown sugar
1 1/2 cups apple juice
4 1/2 cups milk
Chopped almonds to serve

Method:

Place a skillet with butter over medium heat. Add rice when the butter melts and sauté for 3-4 minutes. Transfer into the crockpot.

Add rest of the ingredients except cherries and stir.

Cover and set on Low for 6 hours.

Add cherries and mix well. Add more milk if you find it too dry.

Serve topped with almonds.

8. Shrimp and Artichoke Barley Risotto

Ingredients:
>   1 1/2 cups onions, chopped
>   1 tablespoon olive oil
>   1 1/2 packages (9 ounce each) frozen artichoke hearts, thawed, quartered
>   4 1/2 cups boiling water
>   2 tablespoons Better than Bouillon Lobster Base
>   5 cloves garlic, mined
>   1 1/2 cups pearl barley
>   1 1/2 pounds shrimp, peeled deveined
>   6 ounce baby spinach
>   3 ounce parmesan cheese, grated
>   3 teaspoon lemon zest, grated
>   Freshly ground black pepper to taste

Salt to taste

Method:

Add lobster base to boiling water. Whisk well and keep it aside.

Place a nonstick skillet over low heat. Add oil and onions and sauté till it gets translucent.

Then add garlic and sauté until fragrant. Transfer into the crockpot.

Add lobster base solution and rest of the ingredients except spinach, lemon zest, cheese, and shrimp.

Cover and cook on Low for 6 hours or on High for 3 hours.

During the last 15 minutes of cooking, add shrimp and cheese and stir.

Cover and cook on High for 15 minutes.

Add lemon zest and baby spinach. Mix well. Taste and adjust the seasoning and serve.

9. Cinnamon Swirl Slow cooked Pancake Bake

Ingredients:
- 2 cups Bisquick
- 2/3 cup granulated sugar
- 2 eggs
- 1 cup milk
- 2 tablespoons cinnamon
- Cooking spray

Method:
- 2 cups Bisquick
- 2/3 cup granulated sugar
- 2 eggs
- Cooking spray

Chapter 5: Recipes for Soups and Stews

10. Chicken and Pasta Soup

Ingredients:
- 1 pound chicken thighs
- 2 carrots, cut into 1 inch pieces
- 2 stalks celery, cut into ½ inch pieces
- 1 small onion, halved
- 2 cloves garlic, smashed
- 1 bay leaf
- 1/2 teaspoon kosher salt
- 3 cups water
- Pepper powder to taste
- 1/4 cup small pasta
- 2 tablespoons fresh, flat leaf parsley
- Crackers to serve

Method:

Add all the ingredients except pasta and parsley to the crockpot.

Cover and set on Low for 7-8 hours or on High for 4-5 hours.

Remove the chicken and place in a bowl.

Retain the liquid in the cooker itself. Discard the onion and bay leaf. When cool enough to handle, shred the chicken with a fork and add it to the pot.

Add pasta. Cover and cook for 15 minutes or until pasta is al dente

Add parsley. Cook for 5 minutes more.

Taste and adjust the seasonings if necessary.

Serve hot with crackers.

11. Pork Chop Soup

Ingredients:
- 1 1/2 pounds pork chops / vegetarian crumble for a vegetarian soup
- 5 cups vegetable broth for a vegetarian soup
- 1 1/2 (28 ounce each) cans diced tomatoes
- 1 1/2 cans (6 ounce each) tomato paste
- 1 large onion, chopped
- 1 1/2 cups V8 or vegetable juice
- 6 cloves garlic, minced
- 3 cups shell pasta, uncooked
- 1 1/2 tablespoons dried parsley
- 1 1/2 tablespoons dried basil
- Salt to taste
- Pepper powder to taste
- 1 1/2 cups water
- Shredded cheese to garnish

Method:
Add all the ingredients except pasta and mix well.

Cover and set on Low for about 7 hours or High for about 4 hours.

Add pasta. Mix well, cover and cook until the pasta is al dente.

If you find your soup too thick, add more broth or water.

Taste and adjust the seasonings if necessary.

Serve in individual soup bowls. Garnish with cheese and serve immediately.

12. Lentil Soup

Ingredients:

2 brown onions, finely chopped
4 sticks celery, trimmed, chopped coarsely
2 carrots, peeled, coarsely chopped
2 cloves garlic, crushed
2 rutabaga, peeled, chopped coarsely
1 cup red lentils, rinsed, soaked in water for an hour
4 cans tomatoes, diced
4 cups vegetable stock
6 teaspoons cumin, powdered
2 baguette (French loaf), sliced thinly diagonally
Salt to taste
Pepper powder to taste
2 cups goat cheese, shredded
1/2 cup freshly chopped chives

Method:

Add all the ingredients except goat cheese, chives and baguette to the crockpot and stir.

Cover set on High and cook for 3 hours or on Low for 6-8 hours or the vegetables are tender and the lentil is cooked well.

In a small bowl, add goat cheese and chives. Mix well.

Meanwhile, preheat a grill. Place the sliced baguette on the baking tray. Place the baking tray on the grill. Grill the loaf for 2 minutes or until the sides are golden.

Spread the cheese-chive mixture on the loaf slices. Serve hot with piping hot soup.

13. Creamy Crab Soup

Ingredients:

    3 cups crab meat, flaked, picked
    3 cups half and half or evaporated milk
    3 cups milk
    4 tablespoons dry sherry
    5 tablespoons butter
    4 strips lemon peel
    4 tablespoons cornstarch mixed with 1/2 cup water
    1/4 teaspoon ground nutmeg
    Salt to taste
    Pepper powder to taste
    1 cup crushed crackers

Method:

Add all the ingredients except sherry, crackers and cornstarch to the crockpot and mix well.

Cover and set on Low for about 3 hours.

Add cornstarch mixture and stir. Cook on High for 15-20 minutes.

If you find your soup too thick, add more water. Taste and adjust the seasonings if necessary.

Ladle into soup bowls and serve.

14. Autumn Vegetable Beef Stew

Ingredients:

2 -3 pounds lean stew beef meat, cubed
4 cups beef broth
4 strips bacon, chopped
10 medium potatoes, diced
4 ribs celery, thinly sliced
4 medium carrots, thinly sliced
3 cups rutabaga, chopped
2 large onions, chopped
2 bay leaves
Freshly ground pepper to taste
Salt to taste
1 teaspoon dried rosemary, crushed
4 tablespoons flour mixed with 1/2 cup water
A handful parsley, chopped to garnish

Method:

Place a skillet over medium heat. Add onions, bacon, and beef and sauté for a few minutes until the beef is not pink any more.

Transfer into a crockpot.

Add rest of the ingredients except the flour mixture.

Stir, cover and cook on Low for about 7 hours or on High for 3 1/2 to 4 hours.

Add flour mixture stir well.

Cook on High for 15-20 minutes. Stir, taste and adjust the seasonings if necessary.

Serve in individual soup bowls garnished with parsley.

15. Turkey Chili

Ingredients:

2 1/2 pounds lean ground turkey
30 ounces kidney beans, drain the water and rinse
30 ounces black beans, drain the water and rinse
2 cans (14.5 ounces each) diced tomatoes
1/2 cup warm water
1 large onion, chopped
2 cans (29 ounces each) tomato sauce
1 tablespoon ground cumin
4 tablespoons chili powder or to taste
2 teaspoons garlic powder
Salt and pepper to taste
Cooking spray

Method:

Spray the inside of the crockpot with cooking spray.
Place a skillet over medium heat. Add onion and sauté for a couple of minutes.
Add turkey and sauté until brown. Transfer into the crockpot.
Add rest of the ingredients to the pot. Mix well.
Cover and cook on Low for 6-8 hours or on High for 3-4 hours.

16. Fisherman Stew

Ingredients:

- 1 small white fish filled, deboned
- 6 scallops, cleaned
- 6 shrimp, peeled, deveined
- 6 clams, cleaned
- 6 mussels, cleaned
- 1 medium onion, chopped
- 2 cloves garlic, minced
- 1/2 a 28 ounce can crushed tomatoes with its juice
- 1/2 an 8 ounce can tomato sauce
- 1 green bell pepper, chopped
- 1 hot pepper, chopped
- 2 tablespoons fresh parsley, chopped
- 1/2 teaspoon dried thyme
- 1 teaspoon dried basil
- 1/2 teaspoon dried oregano
- 1/4 teaspoon cayenne pepper
- 1/4 teaspoon paprika

Method:

Add all the ingredients except seafood to the crockpot.

Cover and cook on Low for 4-5 hours or on High for 2-2 1/2 hours.

Add seafood and stir. Taste and adjust the seasonings if necessary.

Cover and cook on High for 30 minutes. Stir in between a couple of times while it is cooking.

Chapter 6: Recipes for Chicken

17. Buffalo Ranch Chicken Sandwiches

Ingredients:

6 chicken breasts, boneless, skinless, thawed if frozen

4 tablespoons buttermilk ranch dressing mix.

15 ounces buffalo sauce

Method:

Add chicken to the crockpot.

Cover and cook on Low for 5-6 hours or on High for 2 1/2 -3 hours or until done.

Drain the liquid that is remaining in the pot.

Mix together rest of the ingredients in a bowl and pour on top of the chicken.

Cover and cook on High for 30 minutes.

Remove the chicken with a slotted spoon. When cool enough to handle, shred with a pair of forks and add it back to the pot and stir

Reheat.

Place chicken over bread or buns.

Serve immediately.

18. Hawaiian Chicken

Ingredients:

3 chicken breasts (about 1 1/4 pounds)
1/2 a 16 ounce can sliced pineapple, drained
1/2 a 15 ounce can mandarin oranges, drained
1/2 teaspoon ground ginger
2 tablespoon lemon juice
2 tablespoons corn starch
4 tablespoons brown sugar
4 tablespoons soy sauce
Salt to taste
Pepper powder to taste
Cooking spray

Method:

Spray the crockpot with cooking spray. Place the chicken breasts in the crockpot.

Whisk together in a bowl, cornstarch, brown sugar, soy sauce, lemon juice, ginger, salt and pepper. Pour this mixture over the chicken.

Place the orange and pineapple slices over the chicken.

Cover and cook on Low for 4 - 5 hours or on High for 2 - 3 hours.

Serve hot.

19. Sweet n Sour Chicken

Ingredients:

6 chicken breasts, skinless, boneless, thawed if frozen

22 ounces canned pineapple chunks

3 green bell peppers, chopped into 1/2 inch squares

1 large onion, chopped into 1/2 inch squares

15 ounces sweet and sour sauce

Method:

Add chicken to the crockpot. Pour only the juice from the pineapple can into the pot.

Cover and cook on Low for 5-6 hours or on High for 2 1/2 -3 hours or until done.

Drain the liquid that is remaining in the pot.

Mix together rest of the ingredients in a bowl and pour on top of the chicken. Stir well.

Cover and cook on High for 30 minutes.

20. Peachy Barbecue Chicken

Ingredients:

1 1/2 pounds chicken drumsticks

1/4 cup peach or apricot preserve

2 fresh peach, cut into wedges

3/4 cup barbecue sauce or more to taste

1 teaspoon yellow mustard

Method:

First broil the chicken drumsticks by placing it 5-6 inches away from the heating element for 15-20 minutes.

Place the chicken drumsticks in the crockpot.

Mix together in a small bowl, peach preserve, BBQ sauce and mustard.

Pour over the chicken. Mix well as to coat all the pieces.

Cover and cook on Low for 3-4 hours or on High for 1 1/2-2 hours.

Serve hot garnished with peaches.

21. Chicken Curry in a Hurry

Ingredients:

    3 pounds chicken thighs, skinless
    2 packages (16 ounces each) frozen stew vegetables
    2 cans (10 3/4 ounces each) condensed cream of potato soup
    Salt and pepper to taste
    A handful fresh cilantro to garnish
    4 teaspoons curry powder

Method:

    Spray the crockpot with cooking spray.
    Place the vegetables in the crockpot. Place the chicken over the vegetables.
    Season with salt, and pepper.
    Mix together in a bowl soup and curry powder and pour over the chicken.
    Cover and cook on Low for 6-7 hours or High for 3 - 3 1/2 hours.
    Serve hot garnished with cilantro over hot rice.

Chapter 7: Recipes for Turkey

22. Turkey Casserole

Ingredients:

2 pounds turkey breast tenderloins, chopped into 1 inch pieces

3 cups dried great northern beans, rinsed, soaked in water overnight, drained

2 cans (14 ounces each) chicken broth

4 onions, chopped

2 cans (14 ounces each) diced tomatoes with its liquid

3 cups water

Salt and white pepper powder to taste

1 teaspoon dried thyme leaves

Method:

Add all the ingredients except tomatoes and pepper to the crockpot.

Stir, cover and cook on Low for 8-10 hours or on High for 4-5 hours.

When done, pour the liquid remaining in the crockpot while cooking into a skillet. Place the skillet over medium heat.

Add tomatoes and pepper and stir.

Cover and cook on Low for 30 minutes.

23. Mediterranean Roast Turkey

Ingredients:

2 pound turkey breast, boneless, trimmed
1 cup onions, chopped
1/4 cup julienne cut, oil packed sun dried tomato halves drained
1/4 cup Kalamata olives, pitted
1 teaspoon garlic, minced
1 tablespoon fresh lemon juice
1/2 teaspoon Greek seasoning mix
1/4 teaspoon salt
Freshly ground black pepper powder to taste
1/4 cup fat free, low sodium chicken broth, divided
1 1/2 tablespoons all-purpose flour
A few sprigs of thyme

Method:

Add all the ingredients except flour and half the chicken broth to the crockpot.

Cover and cook on Low for 7 hours.

Mix together flour and remaining broth and pour into the pot.

Stir well, cover and cook on Low for 30 minutes.

Chop the turkey into slices and serve.

24. Sesame Ginger Turkey Wraps

Ingredients:

    2 pounds turkey thighs, skinless
    8 ounces broccoli slaw mix
    1/2 cup bottled sesame ginger stir-fry sauce
    3 green onions, thinly sliced
    6 flour tortillas, warmed
    2 tablespoons water
    Cooking spray

Method:

    Place turkey breast in the crockpot.
    Mix together water and sesame ginger stir fry sauce in a bowl and pour over the turkey breast.
    Cover and cook for 6-7 hours or on High for 3-3 1/2 hours until tender.

Remove the turkey and place on your cutting board. When cool enough to handle, shred the turkey with a pair of forks. Discard the bones. Add the turkey back to the pot. Reheat for 5 minutes.

Add broccoli slaw and stir. Cover and let it sit for 5 minutes.

Place the turkey slaw mixture on the tortillas. Garnish with green onions, wrap and serve.

25. Slow cooked Herby Turkey Breast

Ingredients:

2 small onions, quartered

2 1/2 - 3 pounds bone in whole turkey breast with skin

1 bay leaf

1/2 cup low sodium chicken broth

1/2 tablespoon dried sage

1/2 tablespoon dried rosemary

1/2 tablespoon dried thyme

1 teaspoon onion powder

1 teaspoon garlic powder

1/2 tablespoon corn starch mixed with about 2 tablespoons water

Freshly ground black pepper to taste

Salt to taste

Method:

Place the onion and bay leaf in the crockpot. Place the turkey breast with the breast side down over the onions.

Sprinkle rest of the ingredients except cornstarch.

Cover and cook on Low for 7-8 hours or until done.

Transfer the turkey on to your cutting board.

Strain the liquid and set aside for about 5-7 minutes. Discard the spices and discard the floating fat and add the liquid to a saucepan.

Place the saucepan over medium heat. Cook until slightly thick.

Add the cornstarch mixture and stir constantly until thickened. Pour over the cooked turkey and serve.

26. Turkey Pad Thai

Ingredients:
   1 cup turkey, cubed
   2 scallions, chopped
   1 small onion, sliced
   1/2 cup Napa cabbage, chopped, packed
   1/2 cup Bok Choy, chopped, packed
   1 cup broccoli slaw, packed
   1/4 cup hot water
   2 tablespoons sugar
   1 tablespoon low sodium soy sauce
   1 tablespoon rice vinegar
   1/2 tablespoon chili garlic sauce
   2 tablespoons lime juice
   1/4 cup cilantro
   2 cloves garlic, minced
   Salt to taste
   4 ounce whole wheat linguine, cooked according to instructions on the package

Method:

Add water, sugar, vinegar, and chili garlic sauce and some lime juice. Mix well.

Add turkey and cover the turkey with the sauce mixture. Add rest of the ingredients and mix well.

Cover and cook on Low for 6 hours or on high for 3 hours.

When done, add to the linguini. Toss well. Heat for 8-10 minutes and serve.

Chapter 8: Recipes for Beef

27. Beef Tacos

Ingredients:

    3 pounds beef roast like lean chuck or bottom round

    1 1/2 cans (28 ounces each) diced tomatoes

    1 1/2 cans (10 ounces each) diced chilies

    2 large onions, chopped

    2 cloves garlic, minced

    1 1/2 tablespoons oregano, crushed

    Salt to taste

    1 1/2 tablespoons chili powder

    Whole wheat tortillas as required

    Toppings of your choice like lettuce, tomatoes, cheese etc.

    Cooking spray

Method:

Spray the inside of the crockpot with cooking spray.

Place beef in the crockpot. Add rest of the ingredients except tortillas and toppings.

Cover and cook on Low for 8-10 hours. Discard any fat that is floating on top.

Remove the beef with a slotted spoon and shred with a pair of forks and add it back to the pot. Stir and reheat.

Place tortillas on your work area. Place the beef on it. Place toppings of your choice, roll and serve.

28. Cauliflower Beef

Ingredients:

3/4 pound flank steak, thinly sliced, chopped into 2 inch pieces

1/2 cup vegetable broth

4 cups cauliflower florets

1/3 cup low sodium soy sauce

1/4 cup brown sugar

1/2 tablespoon garlic, minced

1/2 tablespoon sesame oil

1/4 teaspoon red chili flakes or to taste

1 tablespoon corn starch mixed with 2 tablespoons cold water

Salt to taste

Cooking spray

Method:
Spray inside of the crockpot with cooking spray.

Add all the ingredients except cornstarch mixture and cauliflower to the crockpot.

Cover and cook on Low for 4 - 5 hours or on High for 2-3 hours.

Add cauliflower and cornstarch mixture. Mix well.

Cover and cook on Low for 30 -40 minutes.

Mix well and serve hot.

29. Pot Roast

Ingredients:

    2 pounds boneless beef chuck pot roast
    6 ounces packaged mixed dried fruit
    2 teaspoons garlic pepper seasoning
    1/3 cup water
    2 teaspoons cornstarch mixed with 2 tablespoons water
    2 teaspoons finely chopped chipotle peppers in adobo sauce
    Salt to taste

Method:

Mix together salt, garlic pepper seasoning in a bowl and rub it all over the beef.

Place the beef in the crockpot.

Pour water all over the beef. Place fruits and chipotle peppers over it.

Cover and cook on Low for 10-11 hours.

Remove the roast with a slotted spoon and place on a serving platter. Pour the juices into a small pan. Set aside for 10 minutes. Discard the fat that will float on top.

Place the pan over medium heat and bring to the boil.

Add cornstarch mixture stirring constantly. Boil until the gravy is thickened.

Slice the roast. Pour sauce over the roast and serve.

30. Beef Roast

Ingredients:
1 1/2-2 pounds beef chuck roast
4 cloves garlic, minced
3/4 cup strong brewed coffee
Salt and pepper to taste
1 tablespoon cornstarch mixed with 1/4 cup water

Method:
Mix together salt, pepper and garlic in a bowl and rub it all over the beef.
Place the beef in the crockpot.
Pour coffee all over the beef.
Cover and cook on Low for 8-10 hours.
Remove the roast with a slotted spoon and place on a serving platter. Pour the juices into a small pan. Set aside for 10 minutes. Discard the fat that will float on top.
Place the pan over medium heat and bring to the boil.
Add cornstarch mixture stirring constantly. Boil until the gravy is thickened.
Pour over the roast and serve.

Chapter 9: Recipes for Pork

31. Pork Roast

Ingredients:
    1 pound boneless, pork loin roast, browned
    1/2 a 15 ounce can crushed pineapple with its juice
    1 clove garlic, minced
    1/4 to 1/2 cup barbecue sauce or to taste
    2 to 4 tablespoons chili sauce or to taste
    1 teaspoon dried Italian seasoning
    1/4 teaspoon salt
    1/8 teaspoon black pepper powder
    Cooking spray

Method:

Place pork in the crockpot.

Place a saucepan over medium high heat. Add pineapple, sauces, seasoning, garlic, salt and pepper. Bring to the boil.

Lower heat, simmer for a couple of minutes and pour the pineapple mixture over the pork so as to coat well.

Cover and cook on Low for 6 to 8 hours or on High for 3 to 4 hours.

When done, cool for about 15 minutes. Slice and serve.

32. Spicy Pulled Pork

Ingredients:
- 2 pounds pork shoulder roast (boneless or bone- in)
- 1 tablespoon chili flakes or to taste
- 1/2 tablespoon sea salt or to taste
- 1/2 tablespoon brown sugar (optional)
- 1 teaspoon ground cumin
- 1/2 teaspoon cayenne pepper
- 1 teaspoon ground coriander
- 1 teaspoon garlic, minced
- 1/4 teaspoon ground cinnamon

Method:

Mix together in a bowl, all the ingredients except pork.

Rub this mixture all over the pork roast. Refrigerate overnight to marinate.

Place the pork in the crockpot along with all the juices.

Cover and cook on Low for 8- 9 hours or until the meat is coming off the bones.

Now shred the meat with a pair of forks and add it back to the pot.

Reheat and serve hot.

33. Pork Chops

Ingredients:

4 boneless pork loin chops, trimmed of fat, cut into 1 inch thick pieces

1 package (7 ounces) mixed dried fruit

1/2 cup BBQ sauce

1 small red bell pepper, sliced

1 small yellow bell pepper, sliced

Fresh thyme sprigs to garnish

Method:

Place the pork in the crockpot. Sprinkle thyme.

Place fruits and sweet peppers over it. Pour BBQ sauce on top

Cover and cook on Low for 4-5 hours or on High for 2-3 hours.

Remove the roast with a slotted spoon and place on a serving platter. Pour the juices into a small pan. Set aside for 10 minutes. Discard the fat that will float on top.

Place the pan over medium heat and bring to the boil.

Boil until the gravy is thickened.

Pour sauce over the pork and serve.

34. Super Easy Country Style Ribs

Ingredients:

    1 pound country style pork ribs, boneless
    3/4 cup ketchup
    1/4 cup vinegar
    1/4 cup brown sugar
    1/4 teaspoon liquid smoke
    1 teaspoon seasoned salt

Method:

    Add all the ingredients to the crockpot.

    Cover and cook on Low for 10-11 hours or on High for 5-6 hours.

    Remove the ribs with a slotted spoon and place on a serving platter. Pour the juices into a small pan. Set aside for 10 minutes. Discard the fat that will float on top.

    Place the pan over medium heat and bring to the boil.

    Boil until the gravy is thickened.

    Slice the roast. Pour sauce over the roast and serve.

Chapter 10: Recipes for Lamb

35. Lamb with Garlic

Ingredients:
  12 ribs lamb
  2 cups vegetable stock
  1 large carrot, chopped
  10 cloves garlic, minced
  6 pieces (15 cm each) rosemary pieces
  3 tablespoons olive oil
  4 1/2 tablespoons flour mixed with 1/2 cup water
  Salt to taste
  Freshly ground black pepper to taste

Method:

Season lamb with salt and pepper.

Add all the ingredients except flour to the crockpot.

Cover and cook on High for 5-6 hours.

Remove the lamb with a slotted spoon. Pour the liquid in the pot to a saucepan and place over medium heat. Add flour mixture and bring to the boil stirring constantly until thick.

Discard the rosemary. Pour over the lamb and serve.

36. Herbed Lamb

Ingredients:

- 3 pounds lamb roast
- 2 tomatoes, chopped
- 3 carrots, sliced lengthwise
- Juice of 2 lemons
- 1 teaspoon lemon zest
- 2 large yellow onions, chopped
- 2 bay leaves
- 2 tablespoons paprika
- 4 sprigs rosemary
- 2 whole garlic bulbs, cut horizontally
- 1/3 cup white wine (optional)
- 5 cups chicken stock
- 3 tablespoons olive oil
- Salt and pepper to taste

Method:

Mix together in a bowl, half the oil, lemon juice, zest, bay leaves, rosemary, paprika, salt and pepper. Apply this mixture on the lamb. Cover and refrigerate for 5-8 hours to marinate.

Place a large skillet over medium heat. Add remaining oil. Add the lamb and cook until brown. Transfer into the crockpot.

Sauté onions, garlic, carrots and tomatoes in the skillet and transfer into the crockpot.

Add stock and wine. Add a little water if required.

Cover and cook on Low for 6-7 hours.

37. Moroccan Lamb

Ingredients:

    1 whole lamb shank, trimmed of fat
    1 medium onion, chopped
    1 small red bell pepper, chopped
    1/2 a 14 ounce can diced tomatoes
    1/4 cup whole olives, drained
    1/2 cup canned garbanzo beans, rinsed, drained
    1/2 lemon, chopped into pieces
    2 cloves garlic, minced
    1/2 teaspoon sugar
    1/2 teaspoon ground cumin
    1/2 teaspoon ground coriander
    Salt and pepper powder to taste
    1 cup water
    2 teaspoons olive oil
    1 stick cinnamon (about an inch)
    2 tablespoons golden raisins

Method:

Mix together in a bowl, lemon, sugar and salt and set aside.

Season the lamb shank with salt and pepper.

Place a skillet with oil over medium heat. Add lamb shank and brown on all the sides. Remove from the pan and set aside.

To the same pan, add onions, bell pepper and garlic. Sauté for a couple of minutes and transfer into the crockpot.

Add rest of the ingredients except raisins and mix well. Add lamb and coat it with the mixture in the pot.

Cover and cook on Low for 8-9 hours or on High for 4-5 hours.

Half way through cooking, add raisins and the lemon mixture to it. Mix well and cover again.

When done, discard cinnamon and the lemon pieces and serve.

38. Slow Cooked Leg of Lamb

Ingredients:

1 3/4 pound leg of lamb, preferably bone out
2 tablespoons olive oil
1/4 cup lemon juice
4 cloves garlic, crushed
1 teaspoon dried oregano
1/2 teaspoon ground nutmeg
1 teaspoon dried mint leaves
2 tablespoon white vinegar

Method:

Mix together all the ingredients except the lamb, mint, and vinegar in the crockpot.

Place the lamb in the crockpot.

Coat the leg of lamb with this mixture.

Cover and cook on Low for 10-11 hours or on High for 6-8 hours or until the meat is coming off the bone.

Remove the lamb with a slotted spoon. When cool enough to handle, shred the lamb using a pair of forks.

Add it back to the pot and reheat.

Sprinkle vinegar over the meat. Garnish with mint and serve hot.

39. Shredded Lamb

Ingredients:

2 pounds lamb stew meat
6 cloves garlic
6 fresh rosemary sprigs
Salt and freshly ground pepper to taste
2 cups shallots, chopped
2 tablespoons fresh rosemary, chopped
2 tablespoons fresh parsley, chopped
2 teaspoons garlic, minced
1 cup lamb fat
1/2 cup duck fat

Method:

Season lamb with salt and pepper and place in the crockpot.

Pour lamb fat at different places on the lamb. Place garlic and rosemary.

Cover and cook on High for 2-3 hours.

Remove the lamb with a slotted spoon and place on your cutting board. Let the liquid in the pot sit for a while. Discard the fat that is floating on the top along with rosemary.

Shred the lamb with a pair of forks and transfer into a bowl. Add duck fat, salt, pepper, shallots and parsley and mix well.

Chapter 11: Recipes for Seafood

40. Seafood Stew

Ingredients:

    1 cup smoked sausage, cooked, chopped
    12 ounces raw shrimp, peeled, deveined
    1 cup celery, chopped
    2 cans (14 1/2 ounce each) diced tomatoes with green pepper and onion with its liquid
    2 cloves garlic, minced
    1/2 teaspoon dried thyme
    2 teaspoons parsley flakes
    1/2 teaspoon red pepper sauce
    1/2 teaspoon salt or to taste
    1/4 teaspoon pepper powder or to taste
    2 cups hot cooked rice

Method:

Add all the ingredients except seafood and rice to the crockpot.

Cover and cook on Low for 4-5 hours.

When done add the seafood, mix well.

Cover and cook on High for 30 minutes. Stir a couple of times while cooking.

Serve with hot rice.

41. Seafood Curry

Ingredients:
- 1/2 pound haddock fillets, cut into 1 inch pieces
- 1/2 pound raw shrimp, peeled, deveined
- 1/2 a 6 ounce can lump crab meat, drained
- 1/2 a 6 ounce can chopped clams, with its liquid
- 4 ounces clam juice
- 1/2 tablespoon olive oil
- 1 medium onion, chopped
- 3 cloves garlic, minced
- 2 ribs celery, chopped
- 1/2 a 6 ounce can tomato paste
- 1/2 a 28 ounce can diced tomatoes with its liquid
- 1/4 cup white wine
- 1/2 tablespoon red wine vinegar
- 1 teaspoon Italian seasoning
- 1 bay leaf
- 1/4 teaspoon sugar
- 2 tablespoons parsley, chopped
- Salt to taste

Method:

Add all the ingredients except seafood and parsley to the crockpot.

Cover and cook on Low for 3-4 hours.

When done add the seafood, mix well.

Cover and cook on High for 30 minutes. Stir a couple of times while it is cooking.

Discard the bay leaf. Add parsley. Mix well and serve.

42. Tuna Casserole

Ingredients:

4 cans (7 ounces each) tuna, drained
4 cans cream of celery soup
2 packages frozen peas, thawed
2/3 cup chicken broth
1/3 cup buttered bread crumbs or crumbled potato chips
1 1/3 cups milk
20 ounces egg noodles, cook according to the instructions on the package
4 tablespoons dried parsley flakes
Salt to taste
Pepper powder to taste
Cooking spray

Method:

Spray the inside of the crockpot with cooking spray.

Add soup, broth, milk, parsley flakes, peas and tuna to the crockpot. Stir well.

Add noodles and fold gently.

Sprinkle breadcrumbs.

Cover and cook on Low for 5-6 or on High for 3 hours.

43. Crockpot Cheese and Prawns

Ingredients:

4 shallots, finely chopped

1 1/4 cups apple cider or light beer

2 tablespoons butter

12 ounces raw prawns, peeled, rinsed, pat dried

4 teaspoons corn starch

2 1/2 cups Swiss cheese, grated

2 cloves garlic, peeled thinly sliced

1/2 teaspoon hot pepper sauce

Salt to taste

French bread or pretzel to serve

A handful of fresh parsley to garnish

Method:

Place a skillet over medium heat. Add butter. When the butter melts, add shallots and sauté for a few minutes until translucent.

Add prawns and sauté for a couple of minutes. Set aside for a while.

Grease the inside of the pot with a little butter.

Sprinkle garlic over it. Add cheese.

Mix together in a bowl, cornstarch, apple cider and hot pepper sauce. Pour this mixture into the crockpot and stir.

Cover and cook on Low for 1 hour.

Add the prawn shallot mixture and stir.

Cover and cook on Low for 10 minutes.

Stir again and sprinkle parsley over it.

Serve with French bread or pretzels.

Chapter 12: Recipes for Desserts

44. Crunchy Cheesecake

Ingredients:
For the crunch mixture:
- 1/2 cup hazelnuts, chopped
- 1 cup Oreo cookies, crushed
- 1/2 cup mini chocolate chips

For the cheesecake:
- 1 1/3 cups Nutella
- 1 teaspoon vanilla
- 4 packages (8 ounces each) cream cheese, softened
- 4 eggs

For garnishing (optional):
- Whipped cream or whipped topping as required
- 1/2 cup crushed Oreo cookies
- 1/2 cup hazelnuts, chopped
- 1/4 cup mini chocolate chips
- Chocolate syrup to drizzle

Method:

To make the crunch mixture: Mix together in a bowl, crushed cookies, hazelnuts and chocolate chips and set aside.

To make the cheesecake: Add cream cheese, Nutella, eggs, and vanilla to the mixing bowl and beat with an electric mixer on medium speed. Beat until well combined.

Take 12 glass-canning jars. Divide and place half the crunch mixture into the jars. Divide and spoon in half the cheesecake mixture over the crunch mixture layer.

Repeat the layers with the remaining half crunch mixture and cheesecake mixture. Do not fill more than 2/3 the jar.

Fill the bottom of the crockpot with about 1 inch water. Place the canning jars in it. If it all does not fit at a time, then cook in batches.

Cover and cook on High for 1 1/2 -2 hours.

Cool completely.

Cover and chill in the refrigerator.

Garnish with the toppings. Drizzle chocolate syrup and serve.

45. Chocolate Pudding Cake

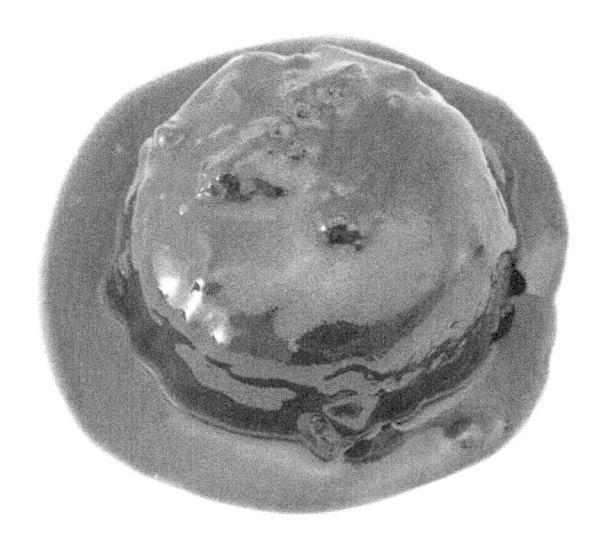

Ingredients:

3/4 cup cocoa
2 cups all-purpose flour
4 teaspoons baking powder
2 teaspoons vanilla extract
1/2 teaspoon salt
4 tablespoons vegetable oil
1 cup sugar
1 1/2 cups brown sugar
3 cups hot water
1 cup milk
Whipped cream to serve (optional)
Cooking spray

Method:

Mix together in a bowl, sugar, 1/4-cup cocoa, baking powder and salt.

Pour milk, oil and vanilla and whisk well until smooth.

Transfer the batter into a greased crockpot.

Mix together brown sugar and remaining cocoa and sprinkle over the batter in the cooker.

Pour hot water but do not mix the contents.

Cover and set the cooker on High for 2 hours. After about 2 hours, a toothpick when inserted at the center of the cake should come out clean.

When done, uncover and let it remain the cooker for at least 30 minutes.

Slice and serve with whipped cream if desired.

46. Blueberry Cake

Ingredients:
- 7 tablespoons sugar
- 2 cups blueberries, fresh or frozen
- 1 teaspoon almond extract
- 1/4 cup water

For dumplings:
- 1 tablespoon butter,
- 1 cup all-purpose flour
- 1/2 teaspoon sugar
- 2 teaspoons baking powder
- 14 teaspoon salt
- 6 tablespoons milk

Method:

Add blueberries, sugar, water and vanilla to the crockpot and mix well.

Cover and cook on High for 2 hours.

Meanwhile make the dumplings as follows: Mix together all the ingredients of the dumpling except milk and mix to get a crumbly texture.

Add milk and mix to get dough that is soft.

After 2 hours of cooking, place spoons full of the dumplings over the blueberry mixture.

Cover and cook again on High for 30 minutes.

Serve warm.

47. Crispy Apples

Ingredients:

8 apples, cored, chopped into cubes
1/2 cup almond flour
1/4 cup shredded coconut
2 tablespoons ground cinnamon
1/2 cup almonds slivered
4 tablespoons ghee, melted
Honey to garnish

Method:

Add almond flour, almonds, coconut, and ground cinnamon to the crockpot. Pour melted ghee. Mix well with your hands to get a crumbly mixture. Press lightly.

Place the apple pieces over the flour mixture. Sprinkle cinnamon.

Cover and cook on Low for 2 - 3 hours.

Garnish with honey and serve.

48. Coconut Rice Pudding

Ingredients:

- 1 cup brown rice
- 4 cups coconut milk or almond milk
- 1 cup coconut sugar
- 2 tablespoons flaxseed meal
- 2 teaspoons vanilla extract
- 3/4 cup raisins
- 2 teaspoons ground cinnamon

Method:

Add all the ingredients in the slow cooker. Mix well.
Cover and set the cooker on Low for 3 hours.
Stir in between a couple of times.
If rice is not cooked, cook for some more time.

49. Pear Caramel Pudding

Ingredients:
   1 cup all-purpose flour
   1/3 cup granulated sugar
   1 tablespoon flaxseed meal
   1 teaspoon baking powder
   A pinch salt
   1/2 teaspoon cinnamon powder
   1/2 cup fat free milk
   2 tablespoons canola oil
   1/4 cup dried pears, snipped
   1/2 cup water
   1/2 cup pear nectar
   6 tablespoons brown sugar
   1 tablespoon butter
   Cooking spray

Method:

Mix together in a bowl flour, granulated sugar, flaxseed meal, and baking powder, cinnamon, and salt.

Add milk and oil. Mix well. Add pears.

Spray the inside of the slow cooker with cooking spray.

Pour the batter into the cooker.

Meanwhile mix together water, pear nectar, brown sugar, and butter in a saucepan. Heat it and bring to a boil. Boil for 2 minutes.

Pour this sugar solution over the batter in the cooker.

Cover and cook on Low for 3 – 31/2 hours.

When done, switch off the cooker. Uncover and let it remain in the cooker for about 45 minutes.

Divide into bowls and serve

50. Tapioca Pudding

Ingredients:

2 cups whole milk
5 tablespoons white sugar or as per taste for sweetness
1 teaspoon vanilla extract
1/4 teaspoon salt
1/4 cup small tapioca pearls
2 egg yolks

Method:

Add milk, sugar, vanilla extract, salt and tapioca pearls to the crockpot.

Stir well until the sugar is completely dissolved.

Cover and cook on High or on Low for 2 hours or on Low and cook for 4 hours. Stir occasionally. Switch off the cooker.

Whisk the yolks well.

Add about 1 tablespoon of the hot pudding into the egg yolks. Mix thoroughly.

Repeat the process of adding the hot pudding mix to the egg yolks until all the pudding is added.

Transfer the contents back to the pot.

Uncover and look on Low for about 5 minutes. Whisk constantly until the pudding is thickened.

Cover and cook on High for 30 minutes or Low and cook for 1 hour.

Top with berries or fruit and serve.

51. Mini Salted Caramel Mocha Cheesecakes

Ingredients:

For mocha cheesecakes:

1 1/2 cups ground chocolate graham crackers or chocolate wafers
2 large eggs
1/2 cup butter, melted
16 ounces cream cheese, softened
2/3 cup sugar
1 teaspoon instant coffee
2 ounces bittersweet chocolate, melted, slightly cooled
1/4 teaspoon salt
1 teaspoon vanilla extract
Cooking spray

For salted caramel:

2 cups packed brown sugar
2 tablespoons vanilla extract
8 tablespoons unsalted butter
1 cup heavy whipping cream
Whipped cream for serving
1 teaspoon salt

Method:

Spray 8 canning jars of 4 ounces each with cooking spray.

Mix together in a bowl crackers and butter. Divide and add to the jars. Press lightly.

Add sugar and cream cheese to a large bowl and beat until smooth.

Add eggs, chocolate, vanilla, coffee and salt and beat again. Pour into the jars (up to 3/4).

Place the jars in the crockpot. Pour warm water all around the jars. The jars should be covered up to 3/4 with water.

Cover and cook on High for 1 1/2 hours or until set. Cool and refrigerate for a couple of hours.

Meanwhile, make the salted caramel as follows: Place a heavy bottomed saucepan over medium heat. Add butter, brown sugar, cream and salt. Stir constantly and cook until well blended.

Add vanilla and simmer for a minute. Remove from heat and cool.

Spoon salted caramel over the cheesecake. Top with whipped cream and serve.

Final Words

Thank you for purchasing the book.

This book contains all the information you will need to get you started with using a crockpot. There are certain tips and tricks that have been given in this book that will aid you on your journey to using a crock-pot. There are close to 50 recipes in High Protein recipes that have been described in the book, which will give you an idea, on how easy it is to use a crockpot to make delicious food for your family everyday.

Happy cooking!

Made in United States
North Haven, CT
28 August 2023